BEYOND THE WINDOW

Dea OZ.
Pleas eyoy the
[signature]
Alan

Alan Gillott

Fighting Cock Press

Published by
Fighting Cock Press
45 Middlethorpe Drive
York, YO24 1NA

Editor: Pauline Kirk

ISBN 978-0-906744-38-3

Printed and bound in the USA by ECPrinting.com

Original Fighting Cock logo by Stanley Chapman

Typeset and layout design by Pauline Kirk

Cover photograph and design by Alan Gillott
Window designed and dressed by Celia Hammond

Author's note

I was delighted to be invited by Pauline Kirk to put together this collection of poetry, and even more delighted when she offered to select and edit the poems to be included, thus relieving me of the burden of *choosing*. None the less, after handing over a pile of material I deemed publishable, Pauline kept asking for pieces I had omitted from that already incredibly long list. Thank you, Pauline, for your persistence and patience.

This collection does to some extent document a personal journey, though the poems are not in chronological order, in some cases, wildly out of place, but they do form a progression. Pauline did not have the dates they were written to hand when she compiled the first cut but she was remarkably accurate none the less. Authors of weighty novels often describe how the journey of writing takes them to places they never planned to go, and I find too, in a scant few lines, that the ending of a poem is never quite what I expected and that the poem touches on issues that were never quite intended.

A poem should not be proscriptive and should allow the reader to, to some degree, read the poem they want to hear rather than the poem I wrote. Feel free to interpret these poems in the context of your lives and enjoy my occasionally twisted sense of humour.

AG

Contents

*To Rose, who has made so much possible,
and to Alex and Stefan of whom I see far too little.
My thanks are also due to the late Alasdair Aston and to
Harry Ellison of New York, who both have had a profound
influence on the way I write.*

Summer

It is almost possible
This summer
To believe I am in England
Where it rains until July
And then some more
Not quite hot enough
To be Humid
And the grass
Which should be brown
By now: a vivid green

I hear the sounds
Of children's voices
The wind in the trees
Even bat on ball
Though not that click
Of leather and willow
Played out with tea
Cake and sandwiches

The songbirds chatter
To the butterflies
Who slip silently
From tomatoes to clover
Which almost look like daisies
Amongst the occasional dandelion
These though are not finches
Nor thrushes; not skylark
Nor blackbird nor wren

When I awaken
From my idyllic nightmare
Where everything is right
But not quite right
I see the unfenced yards
And siding clad houses

Which make me smile
Thinking how close I came
To believe I am in England
This summer
It is almost possible

Norwalk

Dis Location

It is a strange feeling
This feeling of not belonging
Joining in someone else's banter
Knowing that tomorrow I'll be gone
Forgotten in their minds,
Forgotten in their heart.

I feel that I am no stranger
Feeling all my belongings
Apart from someone else's play
For tomorrow I am always here
Remembering all my lives,
Remembering all my heart.

So why then feeling strange:
This feeling to be longing
A part of someone else's stage
Where tomorrow's pace of time is yesterday
Knowing all their parts,
Knowing all by heart.

Chapel Hill/Cary

The A Train

Yes, I take the A train
From Aqueduct to Penn and back I go
For forty minutes to and fro
On New York's famous longest ride
That takes Manhattan in its stride
And I, the A train strain.

Yes, I take the A train
And look, with awe, upon the myriad faces,
Upon the most unusual brew of races,
Who travel in this silver sinuous snake
In whose belly the twin rails take
Me along the A train lane.

Yes, I take the A train.
I've shared my ride with many different folks
Who mostly stand with vacant stare that cloaks
Their interesting inner selves they cannot share
With me, that danger stranger without hair
Who travels on the A train train.

Yes, I take the A train
And given my mighty quarter to the tract
From this cause or that whose needs are wracked
With pain broadcast along this elongated lane
Of frozen temporality, this languorous frame
Who are for us the A train lame.

Yes, I take the A train;
Watched the vendor's chocolate cardboard box
On wheels who's owner picks the locks
Between the cars and s'never seen to sell
His wares: this optimistic tour with bell
This subway store on the A train wain.

Yes, I take the A train
Traveling with nurse and whore, the office bore
This mother, child, and student too, the scores from stores
Who travel up and down with those who deal in crack
Who still rely for travel on this prestigious track
Of New York life: The A train vein.

New York

Quiet Moment

Lost in my inconsequential dreams
Of tangled memories and possibilities
I am aware of you so still and quiet
Reverie and reality woven tranquil teems
With keen relaxed affection
That flows from you so still and quiet

The constant rhythm of your chest
Gently moves my resting hand
Gives life to love so still and quiet
And on your peaceful face at rest
I know you drift serene like me
Entangled thoughts so still and quiet

Together and apart so close we doze
Wisps of vision so alike and unalike
A commonality so still and quiet
Such unexpected trust in our repose
Which daunts our waking cerebration
While yet in truth we are so still and quiet

Greenwich

Shadows of the Bells

I went to school in the shadow of the bells
Sleeping not a hundred feet from where Becket
Met the knights who would shortly cut him down
Walking where the feet of brothers and pilgrims
Have trod for fifteen hundred years
Singing in the crafted stalls they chanted office
Where intoned prayers cling to the clerestory
Even in the eerie silence of a summer night

Forty years on I am back in school
Hard by these less ponderous bells
Learning in buildings no less venerable
Listening to the organ's orchestral chord
Played by the same hands that once played
Those forty years before
Sound settling like the desert sands after a storm
A miasma of medieval minstrel's merry musik
Even in the eerie silence of a summer night

Yet in the echoes of my life I see
Resounding in each provincial see
Future relics of my own to one day revere
Even in the eerie silence of a summer night

York/North Atlantic

Stationary

Three hours ago I called
And the tow truck from triple A
Couldn't or wouldn't find me
Less than half a mile
From the centre of Miami
While I cell' in hand
Stand downstream
In the lee
Of my less than useful vehicle

Rose, on the other hand,
Is stuck in traffic
On the same eye ninety five
But in New York
Now adrift
In the plethora of
Something ninety five
And seventy eights
That riddle Queens
And Long Island

My would be rescuer
Has decided I am too hard to find
Not worth rescuing
Therefore not in his area
(Note I now call him he)
Would I please again call triple A

I do: I am promised a priority dispatch
Priority!
Rain is now falling
On this poem
As I write it
As it did a little while ago
While I wrote another poem
It is getting darker

The lights on this car do not work
Rose is not answering her phone

I begin contemplating
Whether or not it would hurt
If I just walk out into
The carriageway and sit down
In front of the next ugly SUV

It is still raining
It is too dangerous to shelter
In the car we always called
The Grey Ghost
Or should I stand outside
In the lightening
A ready earth
On the exposed and elevated road
Or should I just return
To the carriageway
And wait?

Exit 2D, I95, Miami

A Minute in New York

It is one of those clear crisp winter days
When a beguiling sun warms some other place
That I scramble off the path and clamber
Up upon one of those granite outcrops scattered
So artfully between the glades of Central park

These primeval rocks an imperceptible observer
Of remorseless nature and relentless time
Ground by glacier, wind and incessant rain
Now dwarfed by the surrounding gothic shadows
Of the never silent and ever changing city

For a moment in my mind I freely wander
The numbered streets and up and down the avenues
Hearing the subway growl and rumble underneath
Paved roads green squares and hidden basements
And nowhere do I see a trace of these stalwart stones

I remember how in optimistic youth
My heroes laid the rails and suspended bridges
Blasted ever longer tunnels and filled great fens
Who built great iron ships and cut flights of canals
They founded this city by raising the rocks

Yet I dreamed of an aspiring designer
Shipping enormous stones from afar to this park
And placing one here and one there in no pattern
Just so that I in the sun and the cold could climb
So artfully between the glades of Central park

Norwalk

8

Neverglades

In between the scream of tyres
And the engine roar
Along the Tamiami Trail
There is silence

For a moment
But it is silence
It is that moment
Taken by the
Alligator to make a call
And for another
On the other side of the road
To respond

There is a moment
Of admiration
In their adaptation
Quickly stifled by guilt
Knowing that my car
Is one of those
Screaming along the trail
Drowning the silence
Until there are no more calls
And no more reason
To visit the Everglades
Which will return
To a new more deadly silence
Of nothing
Because there will be no one left
To visit.

Florida Everglades

9

Still

Still, in the moonlight
Glowing silent stirred
By rippling fluster
And rhythmic shore
This peaceful lake
Belies the force
Of feeding streams
And draining river's
Rushing ever churning fall
While deep below the placid
Skein of silver skin
The chain of danger
Feeds life on life
In an Ever changing flow

Still, in the moonlight
Glowing silent stirred
Her rippling chest
And rhythmic breath
Sound perfect peace
Belie the force
Of new cells formed
As others waste away
In churning alimentary fall
While deep below the placid
Skein of perfect skin
The chain of danger
Feeds life on life
In an Ever changing flow

Norwalk

'Plane Beat

Unlike the heartbeat of the train
There is no rhythm in the 'plane
That makes it hard to paint romance
In metered verse and flowing stance

The hurly burly hustle bustle
Of steamship's port side daily tussle
Eclipses far the silent shuffle
Of paging calls and paper rustle

There is no wind or rain or rattle
To kiss the cheek or part the hair
And share the beauty and the battle
Of tempestuous shores and scenic flair

Because from port to port we bound
Cocooned so far above the ground

North America

The Lie

It was a long time ago
The call: so strong; a powerful
Imperative to serve my Lord:
A sacrifice for his people.

Willingly I promised to forgo
The passion of my sex: my full
Being being the passion of my Lord,
My sacrifice, my life, my all.

I've blest; I've counselled;
I've heard confession of sin
No man should hear: which bow
My shoulders and make me weep at night.

Throughout all this I've not rebelled,
I've kept my vows, resolved to win
My place in heaven, my Lord to follow
Turning my face toward his light.

I am no paragon; I've fallen now and then
To thinking how it might have been
To fall for that petite colleen
While indulging in a little self manipulation.

I celebrate the joys of men and women
Preaching conceptual love that's seen
By Holy Church to be the mean
By which to judge the matrimonial situation.

Every day this little facet
Eats away a measure of my heart
Reducing the wellspring of my life
And comes between me and my congregation.

And when I die, this body wracked;
This shrivelled heart will be so far apart
From God: the vow, the knife
That sends me to my condemnation.

Purley

Careless Love

To lose one's heart is a careless act
To surrender all control
To someone else
To give away one's soul

To share one's heart with someone else
Requires a sturdy self control
To let a stranger
Touch the organ of one's soul

Even then as mingling hearts are one
The secret is to keep control
Of every other beat
And in between entwine one's soul

Because once lost, the heart is never found
And never takes control
Again: the secret beat
Will never ever touch the soul

For it is the inner self that counts
Which cannot take control
And breathe a life
Into a heart that's lost its soul

Ozone Park

The Eighth Day

On the morning of the Eighth day
Amidst an unbearable chitter
Of slithering seraphs
And relentless chatter
Of capering cherubim
And the most loathsome of headaches,
Of course assuming that we
In assuming the likeness of god
Can assume that god has a head
And such a head can assume
The theocorporial equivalent of a migraine.

Before looking out over this creation
And proudly exclaiming that it was good
God first regretted the overindulgence
Of nectar and ambrosia
At last night's "We finished the World" party
Noting briefly that it was even worse
Than the one from inducing the Big Bang.

With a swirl of the theocorporial robe
Dispersing the throng of the heavenly host
Throughout the known and unknown universe
God set out to clear the assumptive head
And gloat over the wonderful cre...

Ouch! Oh my! God thought
Woe is me, alack-a-day
This being the theomental equivalent
Of blasphemous and sexual epithets
As God finally looked out over creation
Seeing the stark reality of giving man dominion
Over the birds of the air and the beasts of the field.

Why? Oh! Why did I petulantly ignore Lucifer's
Most insistent nagging to allow mankind
Be only stewards of this creation
Whose resources are almost gone
And the bewildering array of fascinating creatures
That had taken eons of tinkering
Vanishing as fast as the poisonous
Emanations of this foul creature overwhelm the globe.

And where on earth had the platform of presumptive preachers
Gotten the idea they could assume the voice of God
And prophesy in "His" name
Assuming an inappropriate masculinity
For a deity who had considerable fun
In the role of Belili, Venus and the moon in all her aspects

And by what incredible authority
Did they advocate the subjugation
Of women and torment of children
The repression of the weak
Oppression of the meek
And tyranny of a corrupt priesthood
Which had this notion that they were just like God.

God Sighed!
Reaching for the quiver of thunderbolts
"I leave someone else in charge for just one day
And I come back to seven more days hard labour".

Miami Beach

15

Looking At the Shards

Looking at the shards
Reveals so much about
The pot and of the potter
Of how and when the clay
Was fired and colours
Maybe tell you why

Looking at the shards
Confirms the pot is broken
But cannot ever tell if
By Anger or neglect
The why or how or who
Destroyed this thing so fine

Looking at the shards
Devised with crafted care
Of which I write so much about
The pot and of the potter
And weep upon the shattered clay
Of worn and weary colours

Looking at the shards
I never see the man
Or maybe woman who
By accident perchance
Or perfidious design
Destroyed this pot so fine

Looking at the shards
Of human life distraught
I never spare creative thought
For he or she who plainly wrought
Upon the victim only naught
But pain so dearly bought

Looking at the shards
I cannot even throw
The bully's bellied mug
Or paint vile satisfaction
Upon the crazed glazed face
Or fire my kiln of words

That is only ever used for
Looking at the shards

Yale

Skins

I wear a skin from time to time
To be outraged on someone else's part
About the part they're cast to play
By someone else with power seceded
Since I in time have been outcast
Or maybe never quite cast in
I write a script containing parts
With words the player should assert
But don't because their roles are real
And ever fear to touch the power
They cannot feel within

But there are skins I cannot wear
And no script I write can ever tell
About the caste or colour I do not share
Irredeemably black or brown or broken
No hidden well of power within
But only that we must all recede
Returning choice to those denied a say
In destiny or even where to go today
And give them back that part to play
That even I, forefend, have taken, from them, away

North Atlantic

Pan Troglodites

Pan Troglodytes
Is the name we give
To the chimpanzee
That lives in the
Diminishing Forest
Diminishing due to
Pan African policies
By homo not very sapiens

This two legged
Four armed primate
Lives in tribes
Kills neighbours
Uses Tools
And hunts for meat

Pan Troglodytes
Living in trees
Yet ironically named
After cave dwellers
And a strange goat like
Pipe playing god
May soon be promoted
To genus Homo
Homo Pan Troglodytes!
Homo Troglodytes?

But then there's this thought
Of simple demotion
Pan Sapiens?
Pan Non Sapiens

Bethel

Two Days After

Still harbour reflects
Unmoving aircraft
Still unnatural
Silent remembrance

Quiet sky reframes
Distant fighter jets
Quiet contrails ply
Our remonstration

Soaring gull reforms
Unaware of death's
Soaring sad stillness
And angry revenge

Dark sky's stars refine
Raw rage into dawn's
Dark lightening to
Herald forgiveness

Boston

Teaching Tyranny

At school I remember
Teachers missing
Body parts
And most of the men
Enjoyed military rank
Captain, Major, Colonel, Brigadier
Courtesy promotions honouring
The part they played
In defeating Tyranny

Pictures of the maimed and mutilated
Of foreign wars, mostly children,
Marred in my name
Without my permission
Bring sharply to mind
These men reduced
To teaching me
Everything but the value of life
The cost of tyranny and the price
Other people pay to be saved
From the tyrant I paid to torture them

E Croydon

Jobcentre

Islands of gray against the green
And yellow designer dividers
Where eager seekers sit or wait
On square red or blue unexpected soft
Seats or tentatively tap or jab
The computerized job announcements

These tired gray men and women
Weary of laws and government regulation
Their sallow skins contrast
The vibrant décor and keen demeanour
Of the luckless no longer employed
They are paid to shepherd and succour

These dour gray haired, gray eyed, gray skinned
Empty sorts cajole and corral
Encourage and enjoin entering data
From blue green forms on collared screens
With coded cards they guide their clients
Who leave with spirits grayed and weary

Milton Keynes

Thirty-three Years

It only takes a minute does it not
To twist her arm, bend her over,
Push in this powerful manly shot
Soon to forget in youthful clover

But not for her, that careless minute
Taken unconcerned by you
Begins and never ends, an infinite
Taint distorting her contorted view

With one single thrusting stroke you stole
From her her inner sense of worth
Her soul no longer sacred plays a role
She must sustain for life: there's no rebirth

No balm allay that endless blame
No more deserved than your gift to her
Replayed again as you maim with shame
Your heedless deed will every day recur

She was fifteen, a virgin
Walking carefree in the sand
Returning home alone, safe
Along the Vineyard's shore

There were three of you
Brave in one another's frenzy
Feeding on this innocent child
In self congratulatory lust

You got away, she didn't tell
No longer sacred
She tore herself apart:
She no longer cared

This secret little thing
Never shared with those who cared
Who never knew this pain
She housed so close

Who could ever love
This slut who failed
To fight three lustful men
On Vineyard's sunset shore

What did it matter
If she gave herself
To anyone who asked
Who wanted more

What did it matter
If she lived alone
Unable to love
Unable to share

What did it matter
If she could not discern
My love for her
It mattered to me

Yes, I am now your victim after thirty-three slow years
Deep inside this lonely soul who lived so much alone
I found that carefree sinless girl and shared her fears
I touched the beauty she could not see and drew from stone
That essential loving teen she should have been

Those times I knew she yearned so much for me
Warm against my skin throughout the night
Her love unacknowledged thus plain to see
And with many other things so clearly right
I risked my heart for her without demur

But trust is dearly bought, the price too high
Redeeming all those years alone, she could not share
That space around her sheltered soul: too close a tie
To risk her still unworthy self with anyone to dare
The safer play was to send me away

Canondale

I Can't Get Away

I remember your face
From Jack's music store
You stood by the case
Of songs I adore

I can't get away from that image of you
That fills up my mind, but leaves me no clue
Of who you really are and what you really do
For if I knew you my love I'll renew

I remember your voice
In Jack's music shop
As you made your choice
I came to a stop

I can't get away from that image of you
That fills up my mind, but leaves me no clue
Of who you really are and what you really do
I wish you could call: my love I'll renew

I remember your eyes
At Jack's music treat
So womanly wise
Like songs to me sweet

I can't get away from that image of you
That fills up my mind, but leaves me no clue
Of who you really are and what you really do
So just for your smile my love I'll renew

I remember your hair
At Jack's music fair
Your sweetness so rare
I could only stare

I can't get away from that image of you
That fills up my mind, but leaves me no clue
Of who you really are and what you really do
For a brush of your hair my love I'll renew

I remember you last
As you left the street
You floated right past
Me hoping we'd meet

I can't get away from that image of you
That fills up my mind, but leaves me no clue
Of who you really are and what you really do
If you'd notice me - my love I'll renew

I can't get away from that image of you
That fills up my mind, but leaves me no clue
Of who you really are and what you really do
That even apart my love I'll renew

New Jersey

Sleeping On the Porch

Sleeping, or not, on the porch
I watch the night sky
Blurred by imperfect eyes
Through the glass ceiling
And the long past lopping oak
Pondering why I seem to have
So many bones

She, asleep, or not, by my side
Wearied by Lyme
Bad tenants, a teenage daughter
Too many cats and me, breathes
Three times to my every breath
While even unconscious ponders
Whether tonight's the night
The Lyme will let her sleep

Awake, or not, together
Indigo turns blue
Heat blankets and a desperate need
Not to wake each other
While memories and expectations
Of sweet carnal oneness
Keeps us close trusting in sleep, or not,
As we trust so absolutely in life
And when morning comes we merge
Sloughing night's caution
Priming the primeval pump
That together we can be apart
To face the day again

Norwalk

Walls

I sit among the cooing doves
Manicured paths and weeping willows
Yet I see only walls built of air
And mortared with paperwork

There by the butterfly
A portcullis beckons
Enter here:

But here is another wall
And another:

Not even prayers will fit
The cracks to unlock tears
So artfully cast on my behalf
By the lime green willows
And browning chestnut

These tears walled up
Because to cry is to admit despair
As brick by invisible brick
I find my way home

                                        Bletchley

Daffodils

Today, in church,
The little ones
And maybe not so little ones
Were given flowers,
Almost blooming daffodils,
To give in love
To those who mothered them

My heart broke
for the mother so far away
and our unopened daffodil
to whom I so much needed
to give this simple bloom
and that heart

S Croydon

Ring of Brodgar

These lonely stones stand witness
to a love so strong
that a whole people
moved a mountain
that we would forever know
not what or why or who
but just how much they loved
in a land where lived so few:
I too would move these stones
for you

York

28

I Do Not Know You

I do not know you
My unformed child
Nor will I ever know
Your sex or size
The colour of your hair
And eyes
Will be for ever never known
Yet when we count our children
You will be there
Listed with the honours
Of the living
Amongst whom you tried
So hard to be

I will for ever wonder
Whether - from this man
Who makes boys
Or this woman, girls
You were a boy or a girl
Were brown or blonde
I know you would be tall
And in my mind's eye
I see my boys
Rose's girls
Merged into one
Fine strong
Child

I do not know you
My unformed child
But in my mind's eye
I do

Brickell Point, Miami

29

Momentary Couple

That momentary moment
Preceding the moment
Where uncertain of certainty
Quells certain uncertainty
Compressed in a moment
Is the turn of a moment
Where force and momentum
Makes a couple a couple
Like a polarized magnet's
Uncertain polarity
It's not 'till that moment
You bring them together
For whether they'll join
Or whether repel
It's not 'till that moment
That either can tell.

New Jersey

Pictures in an Indian Restaurant

She turns smiling
Red sari glowing in the radiant
Sunshine, her driverless trishaw
Number five nine two waiting

Light is failing
Coat glowing, the evening
Tiger's unintended menace
Pads by the almost silent stream

Sitar lady posed
Demanding to be heard
Whose easy skills fade
Into eternal nothing

Disguised by shadows
Nets akimbo in the shallows
The village fishes unconcerned
By watchful buffalo

Scattered amongst the tea
Colourful saris and spare leaved trees
Relieve the dense green shrub
Baskets like flowers in a fantasy garden

Amongst the beds
Of yellow linen and rice
Blooms of red wine consume
Unconcerned diners

A Taste of Bengal, S Croydon

Taphonomy

Today, laid on a box that serves it as a plinth
Isolated with due care from my poisoned emanations
And from the ultraviolet by armoured special glass
A label here and there to tell me what it is
And why it's here before me and not laid acid free
Down Below
And I'm left to ponder if the words I read are true
Or a guess made up because nobody really knows
Yet this pretty shiny object makes the people come
And justify this thing for being here

Yesterday, its box was thrust behind some bedding
Isolated with due care from the mistress' perturbations
Because slaves were not allowed to have these little trinkets
Shiny nothings that were guarded with extreme irrational love
These little acts of protest that retained some human pride
Down below
So secret that no words describe this little trinket
And of its type there are no other samples
Yet its value overwhelms the power of any god
And justifies this thing for being here

Tomorrow, laid amongst remains from many ages
Isolated once again within the layered earth
Exposed with questing care by gently scraping trowel
Bagged and tagged in context by stratified location
This curious trinket bared is raised from
Down below
Yet makes no sense where found amongst these other curious
                                                        things
Of many different times and places yet it's so astonishing
It's taken as authentic with a fabricated story
Which justifies this thing for being here

Today, laid on a box that serves it as a plinth
Isolated with due care from my poisoned emanations
And from the ultraviolet by armoured special glass
A label here and there to tell me what it is
And why it's here before me and not laid acid free
Down Below
And I'm left to ponder if the words I read are true
Or a guess made up because nobody really knows
Yet this pretty shiny object makes the people come
And justify this thing for being here

York

Of Paintings By Will Barnet

Pausing enraptured time and again
Before paintings of people
Resting or reading in bed
Or in the garden by a bare bough
Accompanied only by a curved cat
Carved in that stillness only
A curled cat can portray

Norwalk

Retratos I
Breath of life

Breathe on me
Stand close
Breathe on me
Give me life
See how I blossom
Stand close
See my face
Observe the detail
Fine lines
Etched in steel
Breathe on me
Talk to me
Ask for me
Close by my face
Notice me
Stand close
Do not move awa...y

Miami Beach

*Photoseriograph and grease on steel disc
By Oscar Muñoz
Pictures of victims of civil and political unrest
in Columbia

India 1
Return to Bombay

I remembered the crowds
Of unkempt urchins, urine
Filled taxis unruly on the street
In Bombay
Unready for the crushing meet
Of shameful human kine
Who live the very shrouds
Of Bombay

I remember well the road
Hard by the sparkling sea
Where I promised never to smoke
In Bombay
Today the pi-dogs broke
The silence of landlocked lee
Reclaimed land and houses sowed
Of Bombay

Clear and distant graying haze
Of newspaper coned roasted peanuts
By the conquering banyan with my ayah
In Bombay
All around the city pariahs
Beggars follow in historic ruts
Clear in a three-year-old's ancient gaze
Of Bombay

Now watching the proto-whore
Immature lips freely bared
Cart-wheeling to her client's bait
In Bombay
Yet sitting awhile under India's Gate
My elder imagination dared
To remember so much to adore
New Bombay

                         ABC No Rio, Manhattan

India 2
Monsoon

The rain opened like clockwork
On the stroke of six A.M.
These sheets of water fall
For ten whole minutes

The rising sun melts a wall
Of humid air, the conduits
Flushed now dry and dusty
Wake the morning haze

The fresh washed jungle's lusty
Blare of morning music's blaze
Peaks and dies as cloying heat
Sets in for the cumbersome day

The ground, now of wet deplete
Is hard and brown, no fine display
Of green among the ruts
As unrelenting sun bears down

At four again the droplets cut
Through the smell of pregnant rain
And form new muddy pools
Atop the hard encrusted earth

In seconds little fish, dark jewels
Glister, cacophonic frogs now stain
The long awaited daylight shower
With rhythmic riveting clangour

The jungle chatters with even' glower
Insects rise where bats soar
As night falls like a theatre curtain
Certain of the finality of day

After the buzz saw flutter remain
Of day, the constant hyena's roar
Echoes as the sheets of lightening
Decorate the dark to entertain
The denizens of night with play
To entice us for the day to stay.

Ozone Park

India 3
Cooke & Kelvey

Cooke and Kelvey, Seventeen jewels
Read the front of my new watch
With expandable silver strap
On my ninth birthday

Following haircut and scalp massage
Toads and mosquitoes watch
With me the lightening sheets
Flay at nine o'clock

Contrast bright-lit night against
Dim shadows of verandah watch
The tropical still bubbles
Of nine swimming angels

Rump a-wagging in lieu of tail
Little My lies unseen to watch
My cake to steal unnoticed
In the ninth of an eye

As evening closes down the sky
The chokidar stands to watch
The black grounds for troubles
Through nine hours of night

Manhattan

Crypel

Going north from Marble Arch
Is the southern end of Watling Street
That Roman road to Verulamium
And Deva: St Albans and Chester
As they are known today

Before reaching Edgeware
And Potters Bar
That place which defines
For Londoner's the beginning
Of the northern wasteland
And the end of civilization
This road bends right
And to the left forks the road
Signed Cripples Crossing

On lonely journeys
In my ancient Ford
My disembodied brain
Probed the origins of such a place
Of crying pilgrims
Crawling over a nearby ford
Or creeping rivulet broached
By a rickety bridge
Redolent of the mystery
Of middle and old English
Magic miracle and mythology - Cry-pel

A community or little ham
Emerging around a hermit's chapel
A manor growing beside the ancient road
As the province of Britannica
Reverts to kingdoms and brigandaries
Mapping their names on a countryside
We still see today
A mere fifteen hundred years or more ago

Driving once again up the Edgeware Road
Circumnavigating roundabouts
Noting new buildings and traffic lights
New models of Vauxhall and Ford
Yellow lines and traffic signs
My heart quickens as I approach
My favorite little hamlet...
Disabled Persons Crossing

S Croydon

Here Is the Man

Here is the man who built Dokan
And the Bospherous Bridge
Who spanned the Humber
And from whose foundations
Rolled billets and blooms
Rail and sleeper
In iron and steel

Yet on a good day he knows that I am me
And tells tales of tunnelling
Under the Forest of Bowland
And of my paddling in rivers in spate
But cannot remember when we last met
Or what we said just a few moments ago

Yet I love this old man
Feet swollen with ulcerous legs
Bowed back and bald pate
Scarred by innumerable falls
Any one of which could carry him away
From me and that image of Grandpa
He has now become
Which in turn no doubt will I
And my sons
Here is the man who built Dokan
And the Bospherous Bridge

S Croydon

Passing Bells

There are no bells here
They toll neither to call the living
nor dispatch the dead
but hang corrupt
remarking no change
ringing mute unmuffled
alternately still and silent
marking each year
from the dawn of measured time
to its imminent demise
celebrating tacit the loss of freedom
and muted dissent
the marriage of oppression and dishonesty
a silent Angelus stilling love
in the empty fields
Empty because the bells
did not toll when the barbarian came
and no one listened
to the tintinnabulation in their hearts
as the captain called bad change
after bad change
until every bell rang down
and there was no further appeal

Aventura

It Wasn't Meant to be Real

It wasn't meant to be real
This wedding hastily arranged
In a tropical island far away
From our home and our friends
But a mere step along the way
To the real reading of vows
Amongst those who remarked
Our meeting in rhythm and rhyme
And our merging together in life
To be so violently torn apart
By the suspicious nature
Of a paranoid government

It wasn't meant to be real
But a step on the path
To getting home to my love
And pulling together
Our shattered family
We two, two boys and a girl
Cast adrift by circumstance
Ill contrived terror
Corrupt governance
And the defiant winds of fate

It wasn't meant to be real
As we careened together
Two recalcitrant writers
On Shakespeare's birthday
Risking two airlines
The weather and mechanical delay
Leaving two whole hours
For Barbadian taxis
Bridgetown traffic
And island civil servants
To have and to hold
That precious license to marry

It wasn't meant to be real
But there in the garden
Of the Palm Court Hotel
With the minister, arranger
And my about to be step-daughter
We were wed
Joined in love, lust and holy matrimony
While St. George slew his dragon
And rescued the maiden
From crocodiles and Lyme
As in our hearts trumpets rang
It wasn't meant to be real
But it was

Mid Atlantic

Aerobatics

Late summer in a churchyard
Where swallows flitter
To the uneven drone of aerobatics
The apparent silence split apart
By a screaming jet flying low
Below the church bell tower
An attack on the nearby medieval pile
Ruined by time as surely as a single missile

Or in the cold of bracing winter in a field
Escorted by spectral rooks
And the same looping twisting diving
Aerobatic murmur while twenty degrees
Before its roar at rooftop height
Another jet skims toward that church and castle
One slip to erase a thousand years

The buzz a memory lost some forty years
Living in school on the chalky cliffs
Of the North Thanet shore
Chipmunk trainers plying
Above the sun glittered coast
As Silver City freighters claw toward the clouds
Their bulbous noses pregnant with cars
Holidaying in France
While Westland Whirlwinds
In bright wasp yellow
Bustle to the aid of careless boaters
Before the paddle steamer from Tower Bridge
Passing from Broadstairs to Margate
Around the Sea Forts
Artifacts of a war just fought
Not quite yet a danger to shipping

And now and again one of those 'planes
We built from Airfix plastic
Glued Gannets, Hurricanes and DC threes
With choice of transfers
Visitors to Manston

Below the windows swallows swifts and house martins
Compete with seagulls against the aerobatic drone
Remembered in the quiet of summer
In a churchyard.

York

Sunday in the Park

It is Sunday and the park
Is bustling: strollers arm in arm
Alone weave amongst the balls
And bicycles, while tiny people
Trip unheeded below the eye
Dressed boldly in spite of fashion
Mothers and Fathers sit anxiously
Ignoring their offspring munching unheeding
The opportune vendor's wares
Gambolling dogs ruminating on the remains.

A busker trumpets not quite in tune airs
Fending away the sound of civilization
Into this fantastic isolation
Where each player appears alone
In a green meadow, a few trees,
A sparkling river
And the appearance of silence.

Kensington

S U B

What were they thinking I wonder
As I watch them clumsily negotiate
Swing doors and those inconvenient little steps
Littered about old fashioned shops
When they bought those S U V class buggies
Almost as big and definitely heavier
Than an old fashioned perambulator
Certainly better defended

I ponder the semblance
To an elderly wicker Bath chair
An ikon now forgotten
That manufacturers keen to capitalize
On a need to own inappropriate oversized vehicles
Have copied for these invalid children
This first symbol of the damage
Their overprotective parents will inflict
When they fail to thrive in the new world disorder
On a hostile planet bereft of power and water
Brought about by these same proud mothers and fathers

London

47

Imperceptible

Please go to position...
Then there is that barely perceptible pause...
You know the one
'The train on platform...
Three...
Will call at..."
Followed by that list of places you never want to visit
Each proceeded by that...
Pause
Barely perceptible maybe
But to me it's just perceptible enough
To send my brain into a very perceptible spin
Just enough to miss enough
Of that vital message
To perceptibly fail
To take me and my baggage to platform...
Twelve...
Now what was I doing?
Oh yes!
I just perceptibly missed the train on platform...
Three...
Or did I fail to make it to position...
Eight...
Fast enough so save precious seconds
Customer Face Time?
Did I fail to mention I have been standing
In this same line now for over 20 minutes
Watching customer after customer
Perceptibly pause after the imperceptible pause
Each adding seconds to the time
Not being served by the counter clerks
Who perceptibly failed to press their button
Just before they were imperceptibly ready
So my wearisome wait is perceptibly longer
By many many...

Imperceptible...
Pauses...
Accumulating throughout the day.
"Please go to position...
Four..."
Now where was I?

York

The Girl Who Fell to Earth

Unbloodied, in a green fractal landscape
She lies still
By the still flooded stream
A still sky reflects the blood red flower
Of absent womanhood
While she reflects
On refracting sunlit pools
And soughing woodland
Games of motherhood
Soon to be replaced by
The blood of making babies
And the bloody consequences
Of keeping them alive
Until they too lie still
Reflecting on the blood red flowers
Of womanhood
Under a still sky
By the still stream
Still, unbloodied in a green fractal landscape

York Schoolhouse Gallery

After a series of photographs 'The Girl Who Fell to Earth' by Joanna Petrie

Faded Dreams

Once the seat of emperors and kings
A home to princes and earls
And more than enough politicians
To sink the fleet of little cogs
That plotted their way up the river
In the course of the Viking traders
From which they were derived
Laden with wool and wares
Guaranteed by adventurous merchants
Tailors and cordwainers
And the cathedra of a see of bishops
Enriched by piety and speculation:
This city of prominence and reputation
Thrived for a thousand years
'Till the mills and furnaces
Of industrial transformation
Drew away the sparkle
Leaving an empty, occasionally glittering,
Dark dank river, a railway,
And chocolate.

Today, passed by somewhere to the right
Of the Great North Road
This old lady serves cakes and chintz
In her faded velvet gown,
Her jewels long gone,
To a steady stream of callers
And in the quiet of the crisp clear night,
Dreams.

York

Busses

Busses come down my street
A street barely wide enough for cars
Whose driver's shiny paint job egos
Crawl by through gaps
Just wide enough for busses.
But not so wide as flaring mirrors
Flying by at just the height
To take the head of any foe

My street is not on a bus route
But on the route from the end of the line
To the depot where in line they wait, snorting
For the wash or to be stowed away
The first driver back going home first

At night my street is a chicane
For contesting busses whose upper decks
Sway from mounting the curb
Just feet away from the terraced homes'
Upper bedroom windows
Silent spectators of this someday deadly race

Busses come down my street
Which is barely wide enough for cars
But not as wide as the flaring mirrors
Which my head knows are just its height
They hurt

York

Drenched

The rain doesn't just fall
But cascades hard and fast
A wall of water
Battering the skylight
And whipping the stone court
Between the brick raised beds
The outdoor furniture
And large plastic pots

Into this day darkened yard
Hopped a large brown bird
Glistening sodden feathers
Pelt plastered
To peck at the grassy cracks
Between the paving

Sated by the unexpected feast
Of rain raised dining
She launched herself
In a flurry of spray
To the top of the wall
To watch

York

Beyond the Window

Long after turning out the lights
And shuffling round and round
Until comfort and companionable warmth
Consumes consciousness for sleep
The sounds of night continue unabated
Beyond the window

Night-time traffic's intermittent pauses
Punctuated by solitary footsteps
Of the homeward bound
Revellers call to one another
Unaware of just how close they are
With irregular words and unsteady directions
Fragments of murmured conversations
Disassociated lives in broad Yorkshire
Cut glass English or broken accents
Carelessly sharing loving indiscretion
Or indiscreetly berating careless partners
For too much drink or too much something else
That must be revealed to the night
And the almost sleepy lovers
Snuggled behind the windows they pass
Seeding dreams or fuelling wakeful fright
As they stumble home in turn
To sleep, to dream, to hear
The sounds of night continue unabated
Beyond the window

York

Supermarket Autumn

It is autumn or fall
A time of crisp optimism
Or a lament to a lost summer
Anticipating a cold and dismal winter
But for me these last few years
Autumn is the time for
Supermarket virgins

Those lost dazed souls
Bewildered and bemused
Weaving up and down the aisles
Little groups of girls rooming together
Doing their first shop as unsure
Of each other as what to buy
Or one night couples venturing out
Uncertainly confident selecting ingredients
Of their first and maybe only meal together
Filling their baskets
With they're not quite sure what
Discovering just how hard
Their mothers worked week in week out
To feed their young appetites
And just how much she spent
Or maybe their father paid
To gratify their pernickety palate
Now abandoned to budgets
And Sainsbury's Basics

As winter approaches the meanderings
Turn to surety and the clusters gel
To couples and singles as the shopping list
Ossifies to a mindless roll
And a beaten path through
The now greening spring aisles.

York

Restoration

Great Britain is fracturing once more
Albeit at the glacial pace
Of political reality
Though it is fun to remember the last time
Brittanicus coalesced into kingdoms
Not dissimilar to those that were there
Before the Romans came;
Northumbria bound by mountains
And the Humber;
Kent; Wessex, Mercia, Anglia
Names still preserved today
Essex, Sussex

But for those of we who live here
Our care is for our vil,
Our ham, our wic
Those parishes so rudely swept away
For district councils and unitary authorities
To strip away our franchise for the land
From those who cared and understood
Who's neighbor sat on councils and witans
Where boundaries were no more than two hours walk
In any direction
They will come back
Restoring to us our love of place
The tranquility of home
The care or cure of the elderly and infirm
This is truly how Britain will be Great once more.

York

Gathered from the Field

The lark, soaring sharp, reverberates
Symbolic of a time and place
As long gone as that lark will be
Captured by the lazy modulation
In a green and pastoral mode

The seasons pass by parishes
Marked by songs of finch and thrush
Hawk and falcon hunt a cotton cloud sky
While that last dying note sounds into silence

The young applaud the singer
And the old the memory
Of a morning chorus so glorious
A richness of atonal polyphonic sound
Serial calls echoed and countered by kind
In wrapped and folded random phrases

Discordant patterns and chromatic keys
Combine a crazy kaleidoscope
Never bettered by the masters of music
Whose flutes and flues fail, flat to the ear
Foiled by the metrics of time and pitch
Eclipsed by a simple song
And a soaring soprano
A minor mode and those birds
Described in words and in air
For that time soon to come
When they'll never ever be heard again

York

Title borrowed from Trevor Hold 1939-2004

Pantomime

Like every small child arriving in London
I looked to the ground, not seeing the wonders,
The monuments and palaces, the towers and architraves,
Awed by Dick Whittington and his prescient
Anthropomorphic cat, I searched the pavements
For even the tiniest speck of gold

Being of an age where the attention span of a gnat
Is a lifetime, mitigated only by ice cream,
Paddle boats on the Serpentine,
And cartoons at Victoria Station
Strange to think that even before television
Bugs, Woody, and Elmer influenced a generation

Ten years later, walking these same streets
One could see a glister of that cherished gold
Find the Lady, streetwalkers tripping amongst families
Ogling the lights in Piccadilly
The clubs and shady bookshops by Soho Square
And rundown offices of indeterminate businesses

The gold is there: there's no doubt of it
But the trick is that it is never to be seen
By any but the alchemists in looming towers
Uttering spells through small print and legal misdirection
Creating that illusion of wealth that is gone
With a flourish through a trapdoor into a poacher's pocket

Like every small child arriving in London
I looked to the ground, not seeing the wonders,
Monuments, palaces, arcane towers and architraves,
Bedazzled by the actors in the Abbeydale Theatre
I never looked for gold again but saw all adults
As the evil baron, the wicked queen, Arbeneezer
And step-mothers never have a chance for redemption.

York

Black Gold and Mucky Brass

Black gold and mucky brass
Took this town in hand
Delving below the furrowed fields
Ridged for ages by proud contented men
And nurturing bountiful women
Feeding the manor monks and market
From the rich alluvial earth
Occasionally with their children
To incomprehensible distant wars
At a time when even York was far away.

These same proud folk then dug deep
Hewed dirty carbonated gold from seam
Uncomprehending
Breathing dust and excreting hills
Of improvident slag
Choking on smoke, marching
To the pithead whistle's shifting beat
Still husbanding children to foreign wars
Where the mechanized harvester reaped their souls
With relentless proud efficiency
'Till the coal ran dry and cost the earth.

These proud and loyal people
Who tilled and hewed, hauled and husbanded,
Spurned by the men with golden brass
Who turned their backs on those who fed them
And left them their vacant legacy:
The hills of dust and an empty market;
Abandoned manors and an impoverished abbey
No mouths to feed with contented pride
But their own with the leavings of an ungrateful state
Left like the dust in inconvenient heaps
Piled amongst the reduced remains
Of black gold and mucky brass.

York

911 Abbydale Road

My nine-eleven is a house
Terraced in a long black line
Of coal soot bricks and stone
Trimmed root square stumped fence
Shorn for the war on tyranny
That engulfed Europe and the world

A painted black front door furnished
With brass and shiny numbers reserved
For weddings and family funerals
Flanked by the coal hole
And passage to the rear
Used by friends and foe alike
Trades and sales, stamps and the co-op
Stomp through to the yard
With outside loo, today's news
Tomorrow's paper stripped and nailed
For hygienic convenience to toilet stall

By the rhubarb stumps and mint grown
For the Sunday roast mutton
The donkey stoned steps
Welcomed all to the kitchen annex
The black range with ever whistling kettle
And deep sink for clothes and crocks alike

Cups of tea, bread and jam
The mutton roast and Yorkshire pudding
Beef and lamb proscribed to ration
Served on the back room rough hewn table
With ministry prescribed utility chairs
Drawn close for convenience
And the two comfortable wings
Focused on the paper drawn hearth
Brass poker toasting forks and scuttle
In front of which the weekly
Nickle zink bath was drawn
With water boiled pot by pot on the range

Where visitors gossiped and children played
With wooden blocks and tin toys
Generation after generation

From here a door down to a common cellar
Running the row from end to end
Where neighbours met mining coal and kindling
Stored with treasure and trash in the damp dark

On the other side, over the stump by the stairs
The cold displays of knickknacks
Of Scarborough and Blackpool
And the little used under tuned piano
Shared with unlit ever ready fire
Against the day the Queen or Mayor came
Or Christmas with aunts uncles songs and cousins
An occasional wedding or christening
And the room, a ritual in itself of
Family solemnity, childish mischief and indulgent scold

Above the stairs two dark cherry rooms
Grave wardrobe and bed head
Guarded chamber pot housing tables
Convenient beside flannel clad beds
Thick wool blankets and tidying quilts
Deterring cold nights and morning cold hot bottles
Deferring the bitter slippered determined stump
Across the black snow crisp yard
Lit by unpolluted frosty stars

The Millhouses tram no longer
Rattles past the Ah! Bisto ads
Crown eggs no longer sorted by the Guinness Toucan
Neighbours no longer call on neighbour
And nine eleven no longer safe haven
In Sheffield seven
From tyranny now engulfing the world
A memory spoiled for war

Sanderstead

Sewerby Village Cricket

It was a classic drive
The padded foreleg
Forward toward the ball
Good backlift bat straight
Cracking the off break
Exactly right
To lift the ball high enough
To soar over the bowler's reaching fingers.

"Yes" from both bats
"Run" echoing from the pavilion boundary
As the two batters sprint:
An ungainly padded waddle.
The field adjusts for the
Anticipated retrieval,
Third slip slipping behind the keeper
Silly mid on crouches facing the bowler
Deep extra cover and mid on
Race, faces raised, towards long off.
The ball, still climbing,
Crosses the bowler's boundary:
The umpire turns to the pavilion
Both arms raised - "Six!"

The field winds down
The batters pause and turn
Walking back to their crease
Crouching fielders rise
Kick out their cramped muscles
The race to the boundary winds down
The scorer tips an exaggerated forelock
The umpire turns and sighs
Groping into the capacious pockets
Of the uniform white coat.

The ball, unaware of the new stasis,
Continues on, dropping now,
Slowed by the eddies of air
On the seam, now in the grip of gravity
The trajectory a perfect arc
From the Sewerby Village
Cliff top pitch
Into the glorious blue salt sea.

The umpire tosses a new ball
To the bowler, turns toward the bat.
The bowler aligns the seam across the grip
And begins to run:
A lost ball no more than a curiosity
At the Sewerby Village cliff top pitch.

York

Alan Gillott was born in Edinburgh at the foot of
Arthur's Seat to a Scottish mother and Yorkshire father
from whence, at the tender age of six weeks, he was
whisked off to live in Bury and from thence the Bowland
Forest. He was educated mainly in Kent while travelling
extensively to Iraq and India. Though he started writing
poetry as a teenager it wasn't until he was living in
Dulwich, South London, that he met and was mentored
by Alasdair Aston who instilled in him a love for form and
the power of performance.

Alan's career took him throughout Europe, back to India
and on to Singapore and Japan, with jobs based in
various locations in the United States: in Pennsylvania,
North Carolina, New York, New Jersey, Connecticut and
Florida. In the USA he began featuring regularly at
poetry venues and founded with his wife, Rose Drew, a
popular open mic in Wilton Connecticut. Together they
began publishing anthologies of their poets' best work
under the imprint of Stairwell Books. Returning to
England, Alan and Rose founded The Spoken Word open
mic; they continue to publish anthologies and collections
as a way of encouraging excellent but otherwise
unpublished writing.

His publications include poems in *The Nightcap Book*,
Blue Dragon Press, *Community of Poets* Issue 20, the
Connecticut Poetry Society's *Long River Run*, Turn of the
River Press' *Wednesday at Curley's* and the University of
Toledo's *Poems for Peace* Project. He has broadcast on
cable TV, pirate radio, Radio Ryedale and Radio York.

Alan is also a musician who has been singing throughout
his life, taking on the duties of Choirmaster at a number
of churches, and where necessary writing the words and

music for pieces to support the often depleted available resources. He has sung with London Welsh Choir, the London Symphony Orchestra Chorus, and at the Catholic basilicas in Brooklyn and Washington DC.

Acknowledgments are due to the following journals and anthologies in which some of these poems have appeared:

'The A Train', *Along the Iron Veins*, Stairwell Books
'A Minute in New York', *YPG Web Site*, Yale Poetry Group
'Still', *Radio Ryedale: Poets Corner*; *The Exhibitionists*, Stairwell Books
'Plane Beat', *Radio Ryedale: Poets Corner*
'Looking At the Shards', *A First Tuesday in Wilton*, Stairwell Books; *Long River Run II*, Connecticut Poetry Society; *Word Salad & Art Chips*, No 4 Autumn 2006, Word Salad
'Two Days After', *Poems for Peace Project*, Poems for Peace
'Teaching Tyranny', *The Exhibitionists*, Stairwell Books; *Wednesdays at Curley's*, Turn of River Press
'Thirty-three Years', *Radio Ryedale: Poets Corner*
'Momentary Couple', *frisson*, Stairwell Books
'Of Paintings By Will Barnet', *Poetic License 21*, Poets Anonymous; *Word Salad & Art Chips*, No 4 Autumn 2006, Word Salad
'Pictures in an Indian Restaurant', *Wednesdays at Curley's,* Turn of River Press; *Word Salad & Art Chips*, No 4 Autumn 2006, Word Salad
'Passing Bells', *The Exhibitionists*, Stairwell Books
'Gathered from the Field', *Radio Ryedale: Poets Corner*

Other publications still available from
Fighting Cock Press

Webbed Skylights of Tall Oaks (anthology),
Ed. Clare Chapman £4.00

After Passchendaele : a Writer's War, Mabel Ferrett
£6.50

Dancing Blues to Skylarks, Mary Sheepshanks
£6.00

Thinning Grapes, Mary Sheepshanks
£6.50

Natural Light, Ian M.Emberson
£3.00

Fighting Cocks –
  Forty Years of Pennine Poets:Spirit and Emotion, Mabel Ferrett
(Ed. P. Kirk) £12.50

Fighting Cocks –
  Forty Years of Pennine Poets:Mind and Body, K.E.Smith
(Ed. P. Kirk) £12.50

Envying the Wild, Pauline Kirk
(Ed. Mabel Ferrett) £5.95

Patterns in the Dark, Mary Sheepshanks
£6.50

Fosdyke and Me And Other Poems, John Gilham
(with Stairwell Books, USA) £6.50

Temporary Safety, Rose Drew £6.50

Dune Fox and Other Poems 1981-2011, Colin Speakman £3.00

www.fightingcockpress.co.uk